JE
~~J/VIV~~
$

VIV*ELO*   Vivelo, Jackie

Mr. Scatter's
magic spell

DUE DATE		4963 10.95	

Mr. Scatter's MAGIC SPELL

Jackie Vivelo
with
illustrations by
Margaret
Chamberlain

DORLING KINDERSLEY

LONDON • NEW YORK • STUTTGART

A DORLING KINDERSLEY BOOK

First American Edition, 1993
2 4 6 8 10 9 7 5 3 1

Published in the United States by
Dorling Kindersley, Inc., 232 Madison Avenue
New York, New York 10016

Library of Congress Cataloging-in-Publication Data

Vivelo, Jackie.
    Mr. Scatter's magic spell / by Jackie Vivelo : illustrated by
Margaret Chamberlain.—1st American ed.
        p. cm.—(Teachers' secrets)
    Summary: An absent-minded school teacher is unrecognized by
his students when he appears before them as the Magnificent
Scarlotti, a world-reknowned magician.
    ISBN 1-56458-201-9
    [1. Teachers—Fiction. 2. Magicians—Fiction. 3. Humorous
stories.] I. Chamberlain, Margaret, ill. II. Title. III. Series.
PZ7.V828Mr   1993
[Fic]—dc20   93-642
                                                CIP
                                                AC

Acknowledgments

The author would like to thank:
Barb Marinak, Reading Specialist, and the students of
West Hanover Elementary, Harrisburg, Pennsylvania,
who offered comments and suggestions.

Also, the teachers and staff of
Wharton Elementary School, Lancaster, Pennsylvania,
whose "secrets" convinced me to write the story.

Color reproduction by DOT Gradations
Printed in Singapore

Everyone in Mr. Scatter's class liked Mr. Scatter, even though lessons were confusing at times.

Peter Scatter was an absentminded teacher. Sometimes he forgot what he was going to say halfway through a sentence.

Leading the pledge of allegiance one morning, he began, "I pledge allegiance to the flag of the United States of America and to … and to …"

The class went on with the pledge, but they could all hear Mr. Scatter saying, "And two times nine is eighteen, and two times ten is twenty, and two times eleven—"

His students had to remind him to dismiss the class at the end of the day. Once he dismissed the class, but forgot to go home himself and they found him asleep at his desk the next morning. The best times were when he didn't call them in from recess.

One morning Mr. Scatter came to school wearing one roller skate and one slipper. On another day, he picked up a banana and tried to erase the chalkboard with it.

Once he forgot he was talking about trade routes to China and told the class, "So after many years in the far east, Marco Polo returned home … returned home …" Then softly, as the last echo of "returned home" died away, they heard him begin to sing, "Home, home, on the range."

You never knew what might happen when Mr. Scatter was teaching.

"What was it we were studying?" he asked one day.

"It's time for the magician," Tony told him.

"Of course, magic! We'll have a lesson on the history of magic."

The class groaned. They couldn't let Mr. Scatter make them miss another special assembly!

7

A few minutes later, Mr. Scatter's class took their seats facing the stage.

WHERE IS MR. SCATTER?

HE PROBABLY FORGOT WE WERE ON OUR WAY TO THE AUDITORIUM AND WENT TO LUNCH INSTEAD!

YEAH, MR. SCATTER IS PROBABLY SITTING ALL ALONE IN THE CAFETERIA RIGHT NOW.

Mr. Scatter **was** all alone, but he wasn't in the cafeteria. He sat in front of a lighted mirror in a small dressing room behind the stage. He carefully applied adhesive to his face and stuck on a long, bushy, pointed beard.

Next he covered his short blond hair with a dark wig. Then he quickly changed into a tuxedo, dropped a black cape with red silk lining over his shoulders, and placed a top hat on his head.

Swirling his cape, he
bowed to the mirror.

"Mr. Scatter,"
he said, "meet the
Magnificent Scarlotti!"

Mrs. Poppenberry, the school principal,
poked her head through the door.

"Are you ready?" she asked. "Yes, I can
see you are. I'll introduce you."

Mrs. Poppenberry walked onto the stage. For today's magic show, she wore a fancy red dress. Looking out at the auditorium, she said, "I'm pleased to introduce the wonderful, astounding, sensational – Magnificent Scarlotti!"

Everyone clapped as the curtains opened to reveal a bearded man in a top hat with a long, red-lined cape. The dashing magician flashed a dazzling white smile.

With a flourish of his left hand, the Magnificent Scarlotti pulled a bouquet of purple and yellow and orange flowers from the air. As the audience looked at them in wonder, the flowers burst into flames.

"Now," said the Magnificent Scarlotti, in a gravelly voice, "I will saw someone in half. May I have a volunteer from the audience?"

Every hand went up, but the magician chose Mrs. Poppenberry, the principal. Mrs. Poppenberry was locked into a box with her head showing at one end and her feet at the other.

The Magnificent Scarlotti waved a saw high above his head and then began to saw the box containing Mrs. Poppenberry into two pieces.

"The box is now separated into two sections," the Magnificent Scarlotti told the students. He pushed one half to one side of the stage and the other half to the opposite side. Mrs. Poppenberry turned her head to look at the students. Mrs. Poppenberry's feet wiggled.

"Are you all right, Mrs. Poppenberry?"

"Yes, yes, but you're wrinkling my dress! Put me back together."

"Of course. Watch as we bring Mrs. Poppenberry back together."

The Magnificent Scarlotti removed his top hat and bowed low. He stood up slowly, looking at his hat. All the students looked at the Magnificent Scarlotti and his hat.

At last the Magnificent Scarlotti said, "For my next magical, monstrous, mysterious trick, I will pull a dozen rabbits from …

MY EMPTY HAT!"

He twirled the hat to show that nothing was inside.

He pushed up his sleeve, then reached into the hat with his bare hand, and pulled out a large, bright red goose egg with white stars on it.

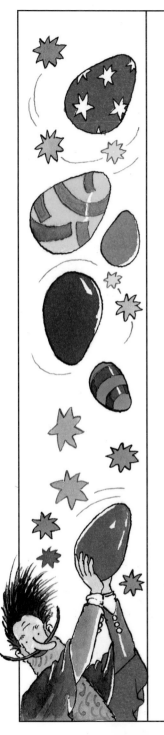

One after another he pulled out a purple duck egg, a blue and yellow egg, and a tiny orange egg.

"One! Two! Three! Four!" he counted. "Keep watching! We'll find a full dozen."

He pulled out a small green and black striped egg.

"Number five!" the audience chanted.

"Number six!" they shouted as a large magenta egg appeared.

The Magnificent Scarlotti held the egg up high. Everyone waited, ready to shout, "Number seven." The magician stood staring at the egg. Finally, with a twitch of his long pointed beard, he turned to the audience.

"My seventh trick!" he cried. "For my seventh trick, I will make this drum disappear!" The magician tapped his hat and the magic hat turned into a drum.

The confused students mumbled.

The Magnificent Scarlotti swung his red-lined cape off his shoulders and dropped it over the drum.

"Now, when I count to three, I will remove the cape and the drum will disappear."

"Where are the rest of the eggs?" asked someone in the second row.

GET ME OUT OF HERE!

"Get me out of here!" called Mrs. Poppenberry's head. But the Magnificent Scarlotti wasn't listening. He was carefully arranging the folds of his cape.

"Say the magic words with me," he told the audience.

"Put me back together!" Mrs. Poppenberry demanded.

"No! No!" The Magnificent Scarlotti said. "**Those** aren't the magic words. Repeat after me:
Simon, flymon, root beer,
Hurcus, spurgus, DISAPPEAR."

Instead of pulling the cape away, the Magnificent Scarlotti looked at the students. He stared at Mr. Scatter's class. For a moment all was silent.

WHERE ARE THE EGGS?

DID THE DRUM DISAPPEAR?

"For my final trick, I will make an elephant appear right here on the West Humbug School stage."

"You didn't make anything **disappear** yet," someone reminded the magnificent magician.

WHAT ABOUT ME?

The Magnificent Scarlotti was
wheeling a huge box onto the stage.

He pushed it in front of
Mrs. Poppenberry, in front of the
hat and eggs, in front of the drum
covered with the red-lined cape.

"The box is empty," the magician
pointed out, "but watch carefully!"

The Magnificent Scarlotti began
folding in the sides of the box,
until only the back was left. Then
he pushed the last partition off the
stage, crying "SOCKO!"

There on the stage was an elephant
with a magician's cape draped
over his back.

Everyone applauded.

Mrs. Poppenberry yelled, "Help!"

The elephant trumpeted.

HELP!

The Magnificent Scarlotti began to bow, then seemed to forget what he was doing and wandered off the stage.

All the students whooped and clapped and shouted and whistled and stomped, but the Magnificent Scarlotti didn't come back.

When they were sure he wasn't coming back, some of the students tried magic words of their own.

ABRACA-POCUS HOCUS-CADABRA!

ZIG, PIG, POP, PUM!

DULA, DABA, BONGA, SHONGA, SNUFF!

IG-LA ZIG-LA BIG-LA BE!

Slowly the students wandered out of the auditorium. No one knew what to do about Mrs. Poppenberry or the elephant.

When Mr. Scatter's class returned to their room, they found their teacher waiting for them.

"You missed it," Joe told him. "The Magnificent Scarlotti was, well, magnificent!"

"Maybe we should continue our lesson on the history of magic," said Mr. Scatter. "Now let's see. The oldest written record of a magic show is from Ancient Egypt. Egypt was ruled by a pharaoh, who was something like an emperor. The emperor …"

"Umm, the Emperor Napoleon was defeated at the Battle of Waterloo."

OH, NO, MR. SCATTER! NOT WATERLOO, MAGIC!

DO YOU KNOW ANY MAGIC WORDS, MR. SCATTER?

"Magic words," echoed
Mr. Scatter. "Oh, of course,
the magic words! Repeat them with me everyone!"

SOCKED OUT,
ROCKED OUT,
ROCKO, SOCKO!

A haze of purple smoke filled the classroom. Everyone, including Mr. Scatter, began to cough.
As the air slowly cleared, the first thing everyone saw was an elephant; the elephant from the magic show.

On the cape on the elephant's back sat Mrs. Poppenberry, the principal, looking surprised. On her lap was a large nest of bunnies, at least a dozen rabbits, all oddly colored. One rabbit was red with white stars. Another one was green and black. These were not like any rabbits the class had seen before.

The drum had disappeared, but a bouquet of purple and yellow and orange flowers was tucked behind the elephant's ear.

The elephant trumpeted.
Mrs. Poppenberry opened her mouth and yelled. The students clapped.

"Everything is here except Scarlotti!" Mark pointed out.

"He probably made himself disappear," said Tony.

"An invisible magician! What a great trick! This is much better than a boring lesson on magic," said Patty.

"It's too bad Mr. Scatter didn't get to see Scarlotti, so he'd know what a **real** magician is like," added Mary Ann.

Mr. Scatter scratched his head and tried to remember what he had been teaching. The elephant reached out with his trunk and grabbed Mr. Scatter's yellow hair, which he had pulled into peaks on top of his head.

"The elephant!" Mr. Scatter exclaimed, as the big animal tugged his hair. "Some elephants," he explained to the students, "come from India, but the ones with the biggest ears come from Africa. This one," he said, happily pointing to its large ear, "is an African elephant!"